Fire Wheel

Akron Series in Poetry

2003 Akron Poetry Prize Winner

Akron Series in Poetry
Elton Glaser, Editor

Fire Wheel

Sharmila Voorakkara

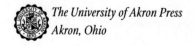

The University of Akron Press
Akron, Ohio

ACKNOWLEDGMENTS
The author wishes to thank the Barbara Deming/Money for Women Fund for an in-
dividual artist grant which helped in the completion of this book. Grateful acknowl-
edgment to the editors of the magazines in which the following poems first appeared:
"Cleaning," *Cumberland Poetry Review*; and "Goat's Head Godhead," *Ploughshares*.

First Edition 2005
09 08 07 06 05 5 4 3 2 1

All inquiries and permissions requests should be addressed to the publisher,
The University of Akron Press, Akron, OH 44325–1703

LIBRARY OF CONGRESS CATALOGING-IN-PUBLICATION DATA
Voorakkara, Sharmila, 1967–
    Fire Wheel / by Sharmila Voorakkara.— 1st ed.
        p.   cm. — (Akron series in poetry)
    Summary: "Collection of original poems by Sharmila Voorakkara"— Provided by
publisher.
        ISBN 1-931968-20-9 (cloth: alk. paper) — ISBN 1-931968-21-7 (pbk. : alk. paper)
        I. Title.   II. Series.
    PS3622.O69F57 2004
    811'.6—DC22

                            2004021384

Manufactured in the United States of America.
The paper used in this publication meets the minimum requirements of American
National Standard for Information Sciences—Permanence of Paper for Printed
Library Materials, ANSI Z39.48–1984. ∞

Cover painting: "Untitled," oil on wood panel, 12" x 16", by Cynthia Hartling, c. 2003

For John and my mother

Contents

Tow

You want some real bad karma, go into the towing business.
—Waitress, overheard

I'm not sentimental. I know enough
to work a man while he's hungry. Promise him a donut,
but save it for later.

I'm not the fast hook that falls from nowhere, but believe me,
when that fist arrives, it's loaded with quarter rolls! Life
is that wind-up without notice—and

wham! No, I'm not given to regret as the chain unwinds
like a woman's perpetual length of hair, then reels in
Buick, Chevy, Olds. In my rearview: a crying wife, screaming kids,

the weedy husband in boxer shorts
running out to *demand*—pigeon chest with baseball bat, a shade
too late. Law says once the hook's in, it's

mine. I'm kept in the dark, which is best.
Good soldier, I have my orders,
and some things I'd rather not confess.

It's not sentiment that makes my little woman pound
the braid of my back, shouting *relax, relax*—but the ache
in my jaw when I think of my kid, pinning live

butterflies to a board, burning down the neighbor's
shed. His teachers tell me he's *tried things*
with the classroom hamster: *Is there anything wrong at home?* Hell,

the small fires that start
a family. I wasn't always this man with bad posture, done in
by antacids and a bed-wetting

boy. God knows, I still believe
the quarter-loaded uppercut counts for something
in the character of a man! *Junior, I'd knock you*

from here as far as straightening—
but wait—
my boy's got something hidden in his hands. . . .

He looks nothing like me. Damned if I know what's mine.
But blood is blood, at least by law, and the word of the law is this:
if you must slit the throat of thine enemy, do it while he's sleeping,

oblivious in his boxer shorts. Tonight,
the apartment block is lit by the rapid fire
of my tow light, light of aneurism and flashback,

that sets this weedy husband in stumbling flight.
Does my heart ache to see you
raise your bat and swing at the air of my remove?

Do I wince at the sound of your wife's sobbing,
at the sight of the twelve kids I wake and strand?
You might recede in the rearview, but believe me,

you will all collect. Revenge is not exact. It isn't sentiment
that moves me forward. No.
I'm watching my back.

The Holy Men of Jersey

By the audible vaudeville of laundry lines,
where the breath of the godhead snaps
bedsheets and girdles, they are called—
thin men—
to the brink
of miracle, to lift light as fog
off their unmown lawns,
to enter
the million-winged midsummer drone in the trees.

The holy men of Jersey ghost
the curtains. Bodiless
as instinct, their thoughts turnpike deep,
deep, where it's brainless and pure
medulla, primal and ancient doom.
They sleep late. Their day jobs grow
cold. They turn in their collars, they levitate

in cellars, they take up nightwork as janitors
instead. Ponderous, clear, they grow
hardly there they are so
pure, wrapped in the evangelical
tentacles of—

what?
What claims their naked bodies as they give up house and car,
as they contemplate the calculus of crows
on the lawn? In the black gestalt that quivers, rises:
they see Shiva, Vishnu, the oilslick arms

of a preaching Jesus,
and the holy men steal away—
strangers.

Their children, grown up, can't put foot
before foot for the holy
tracks them down:
God's
in their coffee cups,
in the chemical spring of their bodies,
in the cities of their bones,

burns blue and luminous, miraculous
as a gas fire raging through
rain.

They never look up.

At any moment, the sky will open
and the birds will pick them clean.

Poem to My Father, Once a Vacuum Cleaner Salesman, Now an Ascetic

Fact: That the dust mites will
colonize, will conquer
the living room shag,

for what is not
food to them?

Smaller than follicle, particle,
what lives beneath
the eye's beholding
shall come forth from the floorboards and

infest, infest, infest! Madame,
I know each low kingdom, phylum,

fungus, spirochete, twister, in its
remote abode. Invisible milliseconds
are lifetimes to them,
for what, madame,

is not desire?

This I remember, imagine,
years on from your six-month
stint, traveling

door-to-door, cold calls,
door in the face or the foot
inside, and you

condemned to spend your days
prowling quota in suburbs, seeking entrance
at the kitchen.

Even now when I hear of some miracle spot remover
on late night TV, I'm made to sit up and listen, to think
of your later transcendence,

to say nothing of your desire
to be clean.

Your ten fingernails grew
pink as a cat's mouth

as you rose from the trappings
of your heavy product sample,
then took begging bowl and martyr cloth,

seeking immolation and
humiliation,
and even *that* was better. In which sage life

will I find you? You should know
that even now I'd like to shed
this plain milk carton of a person

I was born to, go whizzing off into
light or aftermath, that often,

I, too, am struck
by the illuminations off
aluminum siding and wish myself
elsewhere;

that I have followed Moonies, Krishnas, Jehovas, swamis
of Utopian Free Love
to coffee shop chapels
in search of the substance
to lift my shadow;

that I can sit, squat as a Buddha,
at the bus stop for hours

and have yet to find a vehicle
that will take me anywhere;

that *hope*
      and hopeless
                  is the mantra of my breath, as I
walk and walk and am never
born again.

Tin Man

Let me tell you

about daylight hanging
by a rope from late branches;

how the lawn lay down
and died at the doorstep.

How my old man kept grave watch at the canning
plant is an ordinary
story, of no
known moral, only a brief hiccup
in the long shelf life of anger
and sketchy employment,

growing no-shows and

Fuck you. I quit. But

shut up. The dogs in all stories
are at the throat of something bigger
than history
has to offer:

Did hounds hasten at the sound
of his arrival each evening? Did he send out
a blood-whistle to call them to his shadow?

No. No and no and no.
No taste of blood ever entered
the picture, no thread lingered
at the threshold of their lips. Just this:

my father in the guard booth
beneath a punch card of stars,
while the clock dripped

        job

             job

                  job,

and he refined his doctrine of
hemorrhoids, boredom, and postnuclear
endurance. History has no more to offer than my old man
peeing just out of view of surveillance cameras,
and talking loud into the mammoth vats long past closing,
not even a night shift for company, the sound of his footfall

his only comfort, a sound no greater than
himself.

Unless you count the keys—

and who can? Millions jingling on a Saturn ring, and each one meant
to throw an unmarked lock—broom closet,
utility, boiler, and beyond them

black doors to rooms full of barcoded tinned goods—big
as god and just as bombproof, ratproof.

When the stock market crashes, when your money's
no good, what will you have left?

Cans
to be sorted, labeled, sent on many-tendrilled
missions,
nourishment for gourmands
in underground bunkers.

What more do you want?

2

Life is good:

space heater, lunchbox, canned laughter
from the mini-screen TV.
Years later, I have a bigger picture of it all:

the watchman is tiny
against what he watches. On the corporate water tower, a
giant—a blown-up, ordinary
man—dressed, no less,
as a vegetable, a smiling galumph
in vitamin green.

The watchman, less than a mote
in the giant's eye,
has time

to let his teeth go
and his hair begin to weep,

has time to
loosen his belt, sit back and
think, think, think:

how best to beat his wife? With a bent
spoon? A broomstick? His angers

are tiny and
many, have appetite,
and if he demands silence,
puts his fist down in his
castle, dammit, to gag-rule the living
who all around him
conspire—

it's not a lot to ask:

a silent wife and children on tiptoe.
No, it's not a lot to ask.

3

History tells us we all live
to see another day, when the doormat scratches
welcome, welcome
across the dawn-wet soles of his shoes.

No apocalypse, no mushroom,

though my father pulls his sheets high over his head
very much like a frightened man.

History says:
it's the little wars
that kill us.

All afternoon, the trees eat themselves in effigy.

Daylight
blows its brains out,
and so his shift begins.

My Suicide Uncles

Who knows how my suicide uncles
crossed over
the ocean—airborne
on misguided jet streams
or pulled by an earthworm
of black sleeper cars,
to arrive, not
in any Valhalla, but
Philadelphia.

1970:

there were mob hits downtown
and the car bottomed out, and still,
my suicide uncles kept on, kept on, lived
above well-furred pimpdom and Chinese
porn. Who knows where

I'll find them now,
in which hallway, muggy
with nostalgia, gas station, or
convenience store, those uncles
who fell from,
who vanished up

five flights of boarding-house stairs. Now
the ghosts of bachelors in under-
shirts, most swallow-boned and laughingstock
of ghosts, they tell me they can't

take it.

Only two ways to go:
get up or
fall down, and my suicide uncles say

fall down, fall down,
as they did, three
to a bed, so great was their terror
of the harm they would come to.
Each time they visit,

they've grown
another brother
with bad nerves and shaking hands
and complain: *Oh, if only you knew*
the fraud of America,
you'd spit! They're blown

sideways, are snapped at
by blood-sniffing border hounds
in their long migration from bed to the grave

shift: parking decks and motel desks,
to mop down the cities of men's room
facilities. My endless
ancestors smuggle themselves

out of the floorboards, in the smell of old
onions and Barbasol,
to inhabit what they can, namely,

me,
pacing forward, backward, all along the night hall,
punching my legs: *Are you with me*
or not? Answer me!

Listen:

granddaddy roach claws his way up
the drain, flops
on his back
in the white, white heaven of the tub.

Dogs

No one's home but
my father, the night watchman,
sleeping off daylight
in his blinded room. Next door
the invalid veteran, shawled
in the blue cathode of talk shows,
dissolves
in the dark.

Dogs bark in the empty yards;
their gray alarm rattles the chainlink, ricochets off
toolsheds. Perhaps they can see
what wheels overhead
in the blank hemisphere of noon, or what

upsets the bones of midday:
that mongrel loneliness,
one that whimpers, circles the back step,
and begs to be let in.

In a Lost Language

are words for
my father
who spoke
to no one
real, who grew

thin, then unshaven,
then lay down
holy

in the hard ground
of his sleep,
refusing to wake.

A man called
to come undone
is a hand raised
against itself;
is the broken light
of late afternoon;
is this stone
that weighs
on my tongue.

Amanuensis

I

In the wide open white
of a winter field,
my darkness is exactly
the length of me.

Two wings,
stung into flight
from a branch:

a crow so black
it burns.

II

Never his own words
but in his faith-
ful accountant's hand,
my father, that winter,
set down
a whole book—
The Brothers Grimm.

The forest of print
darkened each page, each letter gone over
three, four times:
how a man retraces his steps

to find something lost, to wedge it
safe
in the cage of his mind.

III

When you wind into
the woods,
it's no use leaving crumbs.
The way back's always
pecked blind by birds.

IV

Every word's
a door
torn into a wall.

I walk a slow
circle into earth, over,
over, a zero
at my feet.

The field is a page
that scars,
darkens.

V

Snow on our lawn,
plagued with angels, a shallow

depression
where I fall. I mill
it deeper
into wings, a skirt.

Who is lost
flies into
the ground.

Ophelia among the Fish

Take this hair,
for instance, this cloud of unbridled blonde
which torrent and current
have turned loose from its braid, a lure

for steelhead, pike, the slick wrack
that husbands me—its smug tongue's
my mouthful, now. It seems

years since I was leashed by rushes
and dragged downstream—all my
life, in fact. I've threaded this river, father,
a docile vessel, a sleeve
to its creeping humors.

What name could I have answered to,
once you slipped from me? No one's
daughter, led by the slight of my wrists, christened

by fish, I fell into the easy embrace
of net and trap. How eagerly the moss
bedded me, and the bass nested in my
loveless hollows. Nothing stops

their prying slide, father,
into the keyholes of my eyes; unlocked,
those vacant rooms glitter
with the aftermath of great chrome scales.

Daily, I'm busied
by the water's troubled babble, monologue
that worries me, blank and dumb. Good thing

you're gone—
it's for the best that you don't know
what I offer freely every evening,
the cold I open to.

Saint Breakdown

Picture it:

It's 1942, and my mother, a not-so-good-looking thirty-nine-year-old woman—left,
        by the look of things—
waves a white hankie at the side
of the breakdown, pure white flag of
defeat.

Picture also her two kids screaming in the backseat,
the hood thrown open
on a stupor of smoke as the car gives up
the ghost,

and my mother waits for the kind of stranger whose kindness
brakes,
and no luck, no luck at all.

1942, the smartest thing that woman did
was fall at the feet of moving traffic, to pass out flat
before her vague assailant:
                ex-husband, traveling salesman—
                                random anyone-patron-saint,

and wrap her hands around his ankles.

❋

Dear reader,
if you have never experienced the astral travel of a
desperate woman,

if you have never shut down as you felt
the world unravel, then,
dear reader,

you have no idea how easy it is
to go limp as a sheet, as parachute silk,
to sail right past
your panic
                              or disgrace,
to let wind or arms move you—
                                        what a relief!

Throw up your hands.
Be saved.

☀

But ladies, gentlemen,
that was the pulp of another incarnation, altogether.
Today, as I picked through clearance racks, as I crumpled sale silks
underfoot (having lifted numerous keepsakes
into my roomy bag), I was

approached.

When the bugged men from security
arrived in their two-door
suits, two bruisers in black and oil slick
suits, I knew just what to do:

I fell myself
right down—went limp as a sail or parachute
silk.

*

Credit wanders, chiefly, in the form of heavenly love

and chooses us.

It's not enough
to train your gaze at a tear in the clouds
and ask, ask, with all your might
ask:

Please.

Sometimes, you've got to step yourself
in its well-insured path—

Cadillac, Buick, Benz.

What is not given freely

will arrive in your bag,

and someone, goddamn, will pay.

*

Ladies, gentlemen, you bystanders
on creaking feet,

the angel who sits on your chest
means well.

Remember this:
if asked, claim amnesia.
When all else fails,
scream.

Hitch your skirt high above your waist
and let the sons of bitches blush.

Then let the divine agency of many strangers' hands
move you—heavy,

though innocent, innocent.

Helen of Troy

Beneath a beeswarm of blonde hair,
her brain was a periodic table—
at one point, Lithium,
Barium,
down, down through the chemical
strata of pyramids
and razorblades—at center, pre-
Aztec, pre-
Mayan. Rink music at the boardwalk
makes her weepy for home: there,
that speck, that golden figment of
landfall, the horizon
a humming
sugarbuzz, the one fixed salt
at sea.

Menelaus

If I shook her around
from time to time, who could
blame me? Anyone could tell you
she was crazy, a little cloud of self-
destruct, a gloom of storm
and change. *Helen*, I'd say, *my prize*
pumpkin, my half-wit,
I love you the way
one loves waste
and ruin, the way headlights close in
on collision.

I should have bricked her up
in some unreachable room
alone with her perfume, her
hysterics.

Now I speak to the mirrors that crowd our
vast house. I say: *My little neurotic, my beam*
of negative light, even your absence is demure.

Helen, the mirrors are hungry for your gaze.
All day they dog me with a glumness
I'd like to slap away.

Helen Tells All

In truth, he was
a brute.

Picture it: all day trapped
in a glamorless marriage,
my best years bleeding
away from me—
fast. Lived my life on
automatic, dumb
as a portrait,
an apology haunting
the palace walls,
while I dreamed and hungered

after L.A. : sprawl and Laocoon of rush hour smog
cinching its waist!
Prefab, mirrors, and movie-set
towns. Oh, but I married
down, down.

And Paris? Sweet-smelling wrist
of a boy—(half my age, it's rumored)—
who couldn't love
his love of death? Faint as
sex, it trailed him—risk and sickness,
a pulse, a musk, that I
was plain beside.
What did I have left

in his wake—I,
so easily, willingly
killed?

The first man to terrify you
takes all,
all.

Life with Paris

Tired of watching the horizon
for ships, Helen
drifts, grows uncomfortably
plump. She nitpicks
at dust, runs
a gloved finger over
the room. Nothing
is clean enough.

Paris wearies
of watching her moods,
knows what she is
was always there,
tangled in cobweb, invisible
fishing line she sweeps from her face.
What a
loose confusion of strands! Most days,

she's sloppy as a deflated
lily—her *Oh really?*s and *Golly,
do you mean it?*s, her girlish disbelief
harms him. She is a cauldron of
dead ends and disconnects.

Helen consults the mice. She picks at
the split ends of her hems
and says:
*What, goddamn,
am I supposed to do?
What, goddamn,
is happening here?*

Epilogue

Poor Helen. I hear she's not
well.
She paints
a new mouth next to
her old one. A twin and clownish
mouth, a bitter red and sister
mouth.
Her new mouth speaks,
her old one listens.

And who is this *old self* she keeps hearing about?
Does she rise like the ghost of a previous life
in diner steam? In cigarette smoke?
Her old self,
crammed ominously
in the margins of a closet,
stuffed in a hatbox
or lost. The cunning
of her room
astounds her. All day long,

she pats down the curtains,
peers beneath the sofa,
the armchair. Nothing
stirs. Her new self rakes
the ashes, looking
for bones.

Monologue of the Vanishing Woman

"I am vanishing."
—*Anonymous patient, Brooklyn Hospital, 1993*

Now, suppose I put it to you that I am a half-filled-out woman. What would you do? Would you look at me and say, *oh look, someone forgot to fill out half this woman,* when anybody with eyes could say the same? I don't need an outside observer— doctor or not—to tell me what's naked to myself. And I put it to you that each day the ink grows fainter and (occasionally) the handwriting changes. It slants a little to the right, a little to the left. It's trick ink they're using these days. Trick paper. But, see, here's the form, and I could have sworn that this part is perfectly self-explanatory—name, address, which I remember filling out but can barely read—I believe it's someone else's name now, a forgery, foreign, difficult. I am *not* this person. I put it to you that mistakes can be made, but how is our mail supposed to reach us if all the forms keep changing? And another thing, we all have to go home at night. But whose key will fit which door? And more importantly, whose darkness will we have to enter?

Mercy

They have no memory,
chickens. Sinless,
those innocents slide past the watchmen
of heaven
as easily as grandmother did,
dragging her widowed shadow behind
her.

In life, wrapped in judge's black,
her fog of mourning robes,
she once called each cock by name
to slaughter. One by one they homed into
the gallows of her hands.

I interred her teeth
in a bottom drawer, relics clacking in a
heap
of pencils and spare change. Silver-veined
souvenirs, talk-bones small
as kernels, now
they gnaw
on silence.

In the afterlife's updraft
of hen feathers and dust storms,
grandmother clucks against
the nubs of her gums, worries with her

tongue
the nagging sockets of absence.
And the chickens flock back to her,
amnesiac angels, flying
on the stumps of limbs.

The World's Smallest Woman Speaks

Night after night, I play a packed house
behind glass: heavy breathers
draw open
the slow
curtain of their raincoats
to reveal the glory of their
disheveled selves. They come
to pinch the proof, to gaze at the scale
slant nature allows.

The barker's promised I'm one
hundred percent *alive*, no mirror trick,
no sleight or sleeved illusion, but truth
you can swear by—
blood bone skin hair all real
in the heretic health god himself
intended.

Talk to her and she talks back! Such
folksy pleasantries
in the boondocks! I spend
these vain and venial evenings
filing my nails, crossing,
uncrossing my legs, bored before
the monologuing throngs,
while backcountry women—
well-wishers, all of them—
toss pennies and rub the glass
for luck.

By night's end, I peer
through the smeared blotch
of touch, palm prints of incurables,
gooseflesh pressed to the clear divide.
Barker and I,

we sweep, we toss
what we can: ticket stubs, chicken-scratch
prayers asking the larger-than-life. Me?

I count my miracles
in the diminutive. We split
the profit: cold, mortal coinage.

I pocket what's mine,
what's left.

Talking to Myself

Listen to me:
some days, I stuff my hands so deep
in my pockets just to feel
the lint that bubbles up on the lining, to feel
the nautilus I keep there, a beached ear that plays
the same gray static, simply
to keep
myself from waving
down rush-hour streets, speaking
to no one. At least, I can lace
my mouth shut, unlike

some people: that toxic man downtown
whose voice tears off the sides of buildings
with his wrecking ball litany
of *goddamns* and *mother-*
fuckers. A
menace. Waving, waving his brick-like fists
until the cops tie him down and bag him. Good.

Sometimes, I let it all slide, you know?
I fork straight through
a tin of salmon, linger hungry over stray bones,
fine and prickly as nail parings, fine
fatal hairs in the throat.
The spiny bits still sting
of cold water, sockeye winding through rivers
to spawn. I pick
vertebrae out, mash them up between
my teeth until my mouth's
as clouded and soured as a cat's.

I play solitaire. Lately, I find my address
in any pane of glass,
and I smile myself
well. I breathe,
I affirm: the world loves me.

The mirror talks back, its one empty act.
It smiles and smiles. It says:
I'm better
now.

Bread and Cinderella

Ice in the brain
loves
size six
red satin pumps,
narrow cradle for the stuck-up
arch,

a long-fluted sale shoe,
as in: you could sip
from,

delicate throat
of a shoe.

These ladies, on Saturday, love
the wicked,
impossible-to-possess
clearance shoe, want
a slight and childish branch

of a foot,
would gladly crack
their own toe bones to fit, to fit.

Two black girls in pigtails come up
running,
open their fists:

rhinestones knocked off
sale rack platforms.

Look, gramma,
we got diamonds!

Then loud, loud
all down the aisle,

up from the earth of her black
orthopedics, up from her soles,
she booms:

Ain't no diamonds here,
no glass slippers neither.
Now shut yo' mouf'—
we's gointa
eat.

Audrey, the Laundromat Fury, Says

First off,
no one's clean. But what a democracy
dirt makes!

All day I watch twenty-five triple top loads full on, on, on,
the tantric television
stuck on the same soap opera
station, the same
gray water spin-out and someone's
done wrong by.
The trip of it is:
our sins were never the first.

Picture Eve in her python garden,
who hung out her ten brassieres
to dry. Like any good, bored
housewife, of course,
her mind wandered, Eve,
to whom the branches bowed down,
dripping
with possibility, and whispered: *way out, way out.*
Like every woman, she took the bait
and tasted,
and said:

It don't look good.

I, too, am manmade, born of rib and
rayon, and I'll tell you just what
you're not above:

one day, that black lung of a blowjob of an oscillating fan
gonna send us all
to kingdom come, sure as I'll die and rise
again,

like this Rorschach
of workshirts, these bedsheet
tornadoes, a worn-out rerun on an endless
reel,

sure as I'm driven from corner to corner, condemned for eternity
to circle the joint,
to tell anyone who'll listen
how white my whites, that
there was never any
Paradise,

only this wind, this storm, this snakehouse
of indelicate underthings hung out
and hissing.

I got
Revelation.
I got
disinfectant. I got a Roach Motel
oracle.

I got a million watts of candlelight
for the apocalyptic powerout,
and, honey,
it's all I can do to hold on.

His

Not that anyone ever dared
ask—after all, it was his
business—and my aunt, not pretty
to begin with, but his—

my uncle carved
her face with a kitchen knife. Starting
at the fringe of her hairline, he drew down the length
of her imperfect nose

to the bulge of new-cleft lips
that shaped only *yes* and
yes
from that day on.

He showed her.

What mirror didn't throw back the reminder
of what he could do if
he willed it? And what day passed
when this wound didn't nag him

with its weeping? Its long sobs
tore up his sleep. Across
the scarred acre of her face,
the blade still burned years later;

and where he'd turned up the ground his hand
had mastered—she returned
a welt, a fault—open and sore,
in which she swore

she'd bury him.

The Orchard's Daughter

My father tends the cripple trees.
One summer, he taught me to eat
the soil, bitter as wisdom on my tongue.
I flowered
by the longhand of that seed.

Now winter, by a cold forge deformed,
I gorge my eyes on spines no stake
can straighten. I belong
to the spinster trunks
that corkscrew down.

All afternoon, the white mash underfoot
is cored by crows,
and their cries—pure and ample joy—
are mine.

I Grow Lighter at Night

1

It takes all of me
to get through
these brassy afternoons,
the wide and naked scope
of May.

The hemisphere groans
beneath the long sentence
of days.

2

Business of insects in
the yard: schizoid churches,
hymning, hymning.

The body won't stay
inside:
explosions,
unfoldings, the knitting
of wings!

3

The way dusk starts: thing
on the outside—then suddenly,
a thing our bodies make:
darkness
that leaks from our skin.

Cleaning

Sunday mornings, mother took
sponge and bucket to her prized possessions;

she would not rest, no, not until
she'd rid us of the filth

that she alone could see. She swept out corners
until they echoed; the floors

brimmed with light. Nothing muted
the scrub-cloth's song,

and the kitchen's chrome
shrilled to attention.

How the spoons budded up
her crisped image—over and over

those docile mirrors repeating
in orderly rows: Spotless! Faultless!

Later, she'd take her bristle brush
to me, kneel

and scour until
I bled long, thin tracks.

She swore to undo
what the sun had done, lift

the stubborn shade that clung
to my body, sure she'd correct

our kindred darkness, uncovering
a fair-skinned daughter. Poor

woman, who picked at her own
ugliness, her only dim wish

to perfect, so that even I—scrubbed
and scratched—could bear

the paled, polished reflection
of her love.

Dusk

It's good to be in shadow
like the tree's spine thrown large
on the lawn, its slant
bar, a bone road scar
you follow.

I like how the magnolia's wax leaves
wag and clatter.

In the magnified black,
I'm half
a body,
then none.

Reflections on *Toledo*, Black and White Plate, Page 518 in *The History of Europe*

Yes, El Greco, I completely
agree: we depressives know light's
just the path to something
else—

yes,
I know it in the morning
when the clouds slump
like deep-sea fishes, lungless
bulks bedded on the pins of winter
trees

and
in the stone-in-your-throat
yellow that pines
on each black branch
in spring—what's
opening? *What?*

I know you understand, El Greco:
your Toledo where something holy
opens, where light cracks, pours
revelations of yolk
from above, a stammer
over mountain flanks, landscape of
movement and blemish, and

Toledo remains:
skull of a mountain
on which a spiked cathedral sits

and a small bridge enjambs
a valley's absence. Skinny body, it
remembers.

Toledo is not Toledo
at all, but wax paper greased with diner fat
and smoke—yes,
smoke, for smoke transforms,
makes the brush fire of bushes
in the foreground almost human. El Greco,

you know how light stains,
you know the sky's a Rorschach
ballroom,
the soaked bandanna
of an auto-da-fé—and yes,

the way it rains on grooves and folds in the side
of the hill where Toledo expands
like a memory.
The world is *not*
flat—

or else
where would we have shadow
in which to fall
and convolute?
Here's to the world's corrugations,
accordion folds,
gaps and lapses in the brainfloor.
Here's to its ugly bulges and
biologic! We're allowed

to forget
and what we forget
darkens

until an errant beam of light
threads us
over years and lives
to a place that hurts
when touched:

motherpearl key,
fingerbone bridge.

Luck

—for Joe

One slight second before
impact, luck knocked you flat
on your ass
and sniper fire claimed a rib

instead of your heart. Years home
from the war,

you still pinch thumb
to forefinger, measuring
the fickle millimeter that left you

a little wall-eyed,
but unkillable.

In another life, you would've been
Egyptian, washed and swaddled to rise
and walk from the wreckage
of your body.

Here and now, though, you doctor
bootlegged engines, you
fashion homespun versions of speed in your shed.
The nitroed Camaro, the souped-up GX—

each body's a better failure
to carry you
into small-town legend
by dying:

Tiziano, driven into
the tail-end of a semi; Bruce, whom they had to pry
from the wheel. . . .

But even Death,
stocking-faced cherub,
with his quiver of ill-fated vectors

sometimes misses,
though your love talk coaxes
the needle forward, your life

in the crosshair
of the windshield,

though you press your luck,
foot to the floor.

For the Tattooed Man

Because she broke your heart, *Shannon*'s a badge—
a seven-letter skidmark that scars up
across your chest, a flare of indelible script.
Between *Death or Glory*, and *Mama*, she rages,
scales the trellis of your rib cage;
her red hair swings down to bracket your ankles, whip
up the braid of your backbone, cuff your wrists. She keeps
you sleepless with her afterimage,

and each pinned and martyred limb aches for more.
Her memory wraps you like a vise.
How simple the pain that trails and graces
the length of your body. How it fans, blazes,
writes itself over in the blood's tightening sighs,
bruises into wisdom you have no name for.

The Beneficence of Spinning Bodies

The winter I turned
thirty, I learned
it was easy
to slide off ice slicks,
off overpass and into bank, into the jazz
of oncoming traffic. I learned

that the tire that licks each
salted rut can veer
from its groove in a flash
of self-pity—
if the surface so desires,
if the surface turns
against you.
I'd gone too far

North, and needing something
to hold me, prayed
for traction, took my place
among the freshly pressed and newly
sobered that gathered in strict-backed pews

at church, or the Akron Dry Club—
it didn't matter. Who cared who was God then?
So, months

of brimstone and abstinence bittered
under snow, and our congregations flickered
beneath fluorescent tremens. I bargained for gravity
with the rest of them, swore I could hear each star

eat itself raw
in its very own circle
of hell. *It's fire*

that shapes us, said
shaking hands clasped
around the collapsible neck
of a Styrofoam cup—white and weak
as the flesh
of prayer. Needless to say,
I slipped

out, let
the cold like a charismatic hand
slap the breath back into me:
it's all a matter
of steering.

What loves us
to the ground isn't straight
or sober, but a spinning—
a centrifugal, beneficent
embrace. Earthward—

a little sick—
by the grace of what
dizzies beneath us, we fall,

we stick.

Palmer Method

Smoke that first named you, swirl
of dust,
your name spelled out
in the whip-whirl of birds. There,
the yard's grit, kicked up,
the lathered mouth
of a storm;
funnel clouds thick
in the milkfat scum
of July;

road the hand rounds;
chalk path that bends
back; tail eating
head eating tail.

For Herman, Second Grade

The biggest boy sulks in the back row,
practicing the clutter of letters that become his name.
The yellow paper blackens with what he knows,

which is not much—or so they say. He'll never grow
inside: a dwarf forever in the mind. His lame
stare follows wherever we go. The biggest boy sulks in the back row,

and his sluggish print mows
down the horizon of lines: each letter—a house, whose broken frame
slouches toward the ground. The yellow paper blackens with what he knows:

thunder clouds, weighted with erasure, lower
over the houses' speechless remains.
The biggest boy sulks in the back row.

Brother dead, brother, he recalls, to no
one in particular, forgetting the name
that branches in stone and blackens the yellow paper. What he knows:

earth's plodding dark, the ground new-sown.
It's no use, the letters repeat themselves in vain.
The biggest boy sulks in the back row.
The yellow paper blackens with what he knows.

Mr. Hatpin, Meet Ms. Mannequin

It was early in the days of
computer dating.
Before Technicolor.
Before sequins.

When you could trade in
one limb for another,
no questions asked. Back when

false teeth were false teeth,
and you knew it.

In television studios and churches all across
America,
the hat brim of an eclipse
made its debut appearance.
Night sweats and nostalgia
swept us up
in funnel clouds.

In a house we couldn't afford
to remember, we woke as blank
as babies and almost good
as new. We contrived. We saved
and slaved and built from scratch

by pinprick and black wish,
by stitch by stitch by stitch.

Bridgewalker

I'm not yet
born. I'll wake
my mother—a night
waitress—into song.

Fifty men sleep
in this concrete
Verrazano; their bones pave
the narrows.

I straddle a tear
in the earth. I have no
father.

Between two waters,
my blood's iron-
work, feathers.

Still Life with Falling Garbage

Who made us without
wings? Who made us too
stupid to think up the word

that trips the deadbolt
set against us? Magic word, stuck
on the tongue's tip: *Open up*,

open up. My neighbor's five kids
pound on their door with fists.
Their mother

locked them out. Last night, I listened
to her whip each one to a coarse
red welt: *stupid, ugly*

son of a bitch, then sob: *sorry, sorry,*
sorry. And now she's locked them
out. Until she's good and

ready, hear?
Love lined them up without moving
last night; love makes them hit

with their fists: *open up, open up*.
God has nothing better
to do,

so he makes Astoria
from mud and gull
droppings, from mob hits.

Late summer, the mercy killings start
to stink. Say what you will, but I
was *happy* there,

my window like a TV
with the vertical
off, while fat Glad bags leapt

from upper stories. Astoria,
your sky's unloading its big
ballooned men—Kamikazes

in black crash suits.
They hit the pavement
and split. So I considered

my life back then
a kind of falling: grace
in squalor, squalor

in grace. A drunk gets dangled
by his ankles from the fifth
floor. Spare change

rains from his pockets.
Otherwise,
the usual domestics:

theater of slamming doors
and fists through walls;
dinner plates, underwear,

everything not bolted down
gets thrown.
Me?

I believe
if we just pound hard enough,
hang long enough,

if we are *sorry, sorry,*
sorry,
the hands that kept us helpless

will pull us in—feet
first—will throw back
the deadbolt

at last:
take off your shoes and shut
the fuck up.

It isn't always mercy
lets us in,
but we live—not

by grace, but
tooth and nail, we cling
to that tough firmament.

Kicking the Dog

I

When his wife announced
she was leaving him
for the repo man who
had a job and *real screen potential out West,* .
he wept

for laughing. For three whole years,
he'd been laughing: all
natural and unnatural acts of God—arson, cancer,
collision, star-shaped entry wounds—filled him
with an unbearable urge to snicker. This made it particularly hard

to sell life insurance,
and they had to let him go.

What's so funny? she screamed.

So when the repo man came for the two-story brick colonial, wedding rings,
LA-Z-Boy, nine irons, nineteen-inch color television, his wife and two
teenage daughters, he howled and

snorted, slapped his knees, his sides pinched with furious stitches. . . .

II

1963:

No time left on the clock, two points down and
"Automatic" Jackson's about to author
a sixty-yard field goal—mythic kick
on the fourth down:

> *You do one thing,*
> *boy, you KICK*
> *the goddamn ball, you hear?*

Golden boy, to whom ball meant *missile*,
fires off a shot into the goal post's
spread arms—that far window of heaven—and for one

mother-of-a-moment
that ball
bounced the crossbar, teetered between grace
and damnation
and, and . . .

it went o-
ver, it went
over, it went over!

A certifiable Act of God.

That's when they retired his devil-red jersey.
Amen.

III

Sam, the five-year-old Pomeranian, circles, sniffs
the islands of his shoes,
and Automatic punts him—
fifty yards at least—I mean, that dog is *airborne*.
It smacks against the quarter panel of the repo truck,

and the little gimp hops back on three good legs.
Automatic's moved, deeply moved by such allegiance, his sense
of humor. How he
loves him: Good boy, Goooood boy. . . .

Automatic's fat ringless fingers ruffle his snout and, in thanks, tear the heads off
a few ticks bedded in Sam's panting belly—for old time's sake—before

he dropkicks him. This time, Sam clears
at least four manicured lawns . . . *going, going,*
sailing right off the estates. . . .

The anthem's organ chords hum up over the dark applause of trees.
Automatic's hand feels for his heart, that loyal
old mule, for its kick, its kick—

Same old magic, boy, after all these years.

They Got All-Night Muzak Playing at the Strip Mall

Lullaby beneath
and above you, seeping from unseen
speakers.
To walk there

among the shut shops, the only
ghostly witness
to the catatonia of mannequins,
rigor mortis of ladies'
apparel,

is to thread a chronic
twilight to the single star
of the drug mart, awake,
motherly
from millions
of years ago,

where a woman force-fed you
kisses, stroked
your fevered head,
singing:

Hush, hush—
where we're going, a man
speaks to his fleshtone hands,
and the angels wear cheap suits.

The Transvestite and His Mother

take the front booth every Sunday. Unmistakably
man, baritone,
and a mat of black hair spill
from ruffles of cloudy chiffon.
Around his throat,
plumage swoons
in the gesture of rare bird.
Now and then,
the swans of his hands
reach over,
wipe soup from her chin,
and the shocked fault
of her mouth
strains towards his offered spoon.
At no time
has anyone ever been so hungry
to accept: the folds of her face close
on warmth that shivers down
the living length of her tongue;
speechless, this lover
so overcome by beauty
she's no longer able
to resist.

Brother Zero

Inside me, a moth,
trapped in panicked
orbit, flies up against
the little fact of flesh
to lunge into street lamp
or headlight. Pinhole

by pinhole,
he undoes
the suit of me; soon,
I will not
matter.

Evening sets
his small teeth whirring.

Men in White Suits

Don't tell me the universe isn't
ever-expanding when I can feel
its reverb, its ancient, aberrant
vibrations, when I can feel us
reeling
as we speak. We who ride

this all-night bus, shine
anemic as static beneath a mortal
fluorescence. A convention of graveyard
janitors and watchmen, we're
carried
through darkness. And what's the creak

and buck of this, our ark,
if not a lullaby, a mothering
to our transience? The shut world slips
from our gaze.
                    We have no
station. We are the last of those
condemned to roam—a white noise—
elastic
and senseless
as hope.

On Atlantis

My neighbors drown their
twelve-year-old engine

with a gallon of salt
water. *In-*

surance: loose, sweet drawl
down here where the sea
never reaches, but

colludes. *Not a word,*
he says, but she's
deaf, reads lips,

and won't speak
to strangers, though sometimes

I hear her:
love you love you love you,

her voice like a big, slow
fish.

The walls here are thin. Forgive me.
I listen.

※

Romance is this:

the iron filings of
violin strings;

this bowlegged woman
in black baby doll lace;

the lava lamp ambiance
of his bad wig and mood swings;

the limp she remembers,
or loses.

❈

So the sea leaves us.
Whatever fever it was, pulls down
power lines in its long drag

back. Oh, the heavy
swindle of love

leaves silt and gills
in the gutter.

Last night, he threw
a cake out the window—once,
a cat, but it lived—now

a cake: pink streaks sweet
across pavement.
In the naked

light of day, in frosting, they squat.
The flies make a brutal

lace. He lifts a Styrofoam cup

in a toast:
Baby,
I love you so much, it makes

me sick. And this:
Hey. HEY. LISSEN
to me when I'm talkin' at you.

Freaks

On the lawless fringe of string-lit
fairgrounds, these tented anomalies
attract us:
Ape Girl and Snake Boy, quasimodo
hatchlings love deemed real.
And why not? Why couldn't love

make this
conundrum of limbs, these missing links
in amphibious sleep?

Love,
lonesome, remote,
that slums its lowbrow boundaries,
sometimes climbs on shore:
slick, visceral, half-minded
gimp who always
derails. It ought to happen

more. We grope,
all awe, slow from stall to stall.
In the dark, only desire's
botched logic
guides us.

Man with Baseball Bat

In the small-time,
nothing's divine. Even suffering
takes on a practical
slant: pepper gum and joke
ties; the blunt force affection I work
on parked windshields and rear views,
in love
with the random damage
I wreak:

Oh, the delinquent
brilliance of gems in my wake!
And the metaphysics
of wounded glass—the crackup reeling
from a traceable break! Listen,

the alarms rise, fun house
tremolos behind
the anonymous hits I dish,
and speak to me
alone: *ersatz*
assassin, low-budget thug, you—
minor
blink in the world-at-
large—

it's not size that matters,
but how you talk it up, how
you conjure spectacle
from the chintz you're given.
Little man, it's all in how
you come out
swinging.

Ditch Music

In summer, I'd find antwork
unraveling the lattice
of possum, black thread lacing
the cave of its skull. If I listened,
I could hear the mind loosen
then exit, black jam
of torn and grassy language:
god, god, god.

What I was then:
easily scared, a little bored.
Alone.
And who's to say who was singing?
If I wanted it to stop,
I never said.

Goat's Head Godhead

On First Avenue, first day
of spring and all the manics
are in full bloom! Why,
here comes Donna,
barefoot and down-
jacketed, waving
her fists
in strange allegiance
to the weather
which mirrors us in sudden,
senseless ecstasies!

In windows
of butcher shops,
we catch sight of
ourselves—epiphanies
cradled in the godhead
of a goat's head—believe me,
in the marbled cathedrals of
spring lambs
we exist,

we amplify, we can't
be saved
from elation. We throw our voices
into mansions of air, and they answer us:
Walls of light! Dangerous joy!

The Monologues Men Draw

are a map of
cracks and fissures,
a west-shooting rural route
that splits the thin ice of the continent;
are the tat and loose net
they are always falling through;

are a line cast backward like silk
from their middles: *Clarksburg,*
Fairmont, Morgantown, it was good money
then, a town with one blinking traffic light and
big-mouthed bass.

The monologues men draw
can be read by the gas green of dashboard kryptonite
that lights them crater-faced, greasy,
nose to the wheel;

are lifelines, are rambling, this rope
of talk far into the dark of the lost
plot;

are carved down deep
to the baby skin
of their wrists.

Big Sky, Little Man

Frankly, I admire
the routineness of walls,
the closing off of error,
and the artifice of corners.
In a bound room, a person can breathe. . . .

Clear days, all that blue terror presses
against me—each window frames miles
of breathless vertigo. A
vast emptiness aches to
claim me. A few birds

unnerved from the eaves—look!—their tightening
pinwheels disappear as they peel,
spiral off into a spell
of jittery light that
seizes the rooftops

at noontime. Fear crowds the hour; unrest
overruns the walls. I prefer
a finite paradise I
can fill, containing all
loneliness, in whose

cradle I find comfort:
plumb, arithmetic.

Heaven, friends, is no big-
ger than a pine box.

The Flight of the Insurance Men

They are rightly prophetic; they are
vested. They are executors
of steel-tipped stars and the end.

The sum of their bodies
is smoke.

They leap from sealed windows
without falling, transform into
fire, into flood.

They are the death threat whispered in
snow.

They are God in their clear-headed
fear of the world.

Apology

For the better part of an hour
now, the neighborhood's been drawn
to someone's obscene
aerobic—sex or
grief. Most likely,

the latter.
How do a woman's wails travel
so deeply outside of her? Through wood and brick,
through nebula of asbestos—what dam had to
burst? We're sick, we're
stuck: what to do in the absence

of beating, weapon, or witness?
Whom to call? The Rolodex flips;
the mind riffles each feather-light page in the fat
black book
of emergencies.

An anonymous tip-off brought a cop car cruising:
red, blue, rebound of rescue light
against the building, the siren
cut off, discreetly,
decently. All is silenced for her grand
descent
to the street, descent from sound
to flesh, to wound:

small-boned, startled, in her white robe, flanked by
officers,
to make her fainting exit
in the back of an ambulance.

And we, witnesses, left at the scene,
we're careful not to touch or trundle, to overstep. One wrong move
could cause more harm. Instead,

we take bets on the sidelines:

Hormones? Sick child? Black eye? What?
The story goes running without us,
whisked off in a soundless light.

Dear lady, your grieving made us
famous. Outside of us, at last,
a sound we recognized, and the hairs on our necks stood up,

astonished. Forgive us.

If we stood at our windows, wringing our hands
at safe vantage,
if we killed the lights
to better be unseen,
forgive us.

We are not strong at all, at all.

Emissaries from Other Worlds

Just this evening,
as every cloud arrived
like a crumpled message
in secret text,

a drunk pissed on my front door.
When I answered, he raised
a hand in startled greeting
meant

for someone else. Of course!
he'd accept my invitation to
coffee, a little
television—why not right now?

Illuminated in the black white
of copdrama reruns, the plots speak
to us, intimate and sinister as the story
of our lives. We root

for the underworld; we feel ourselves
pursued. Pinned in
searchlights, we are at last
revealed.

And which of us, numinous
citizens, astral strangers
baring our terror and promise—
which of us isn't
moved to tears?

The Last Nickel Dance

A kiss maybe's as far
as your grimy nickel will get you.
That,

and a wood-hearted
waltz, and the sweep of my long,
dragging hem.

I'm tired,
goddamn.

The orchid on my wrist
shriveled days ago, now
rags out like a tongue. And still

I lead. I lead and I lead and I

wheel the paying men
around the bandstand's shudder
of flowers, while one-handed Sammy

tortures his accordion
into something wounded
and green—*adagio*—

with *feeling*.
Please.

My suitors like
a slow dance, they like
to press up close

and drool.
Love's what you whip 'til
its eyes cross, 'til its brain

pops, then sinks.

Sammy brings on a last,
heartfelt dirge; the accordion
curls and gives up

its ghost.
And my suitors clap
and act as if it'll take them

someplace, as if they could drag out
happiness, that old blue-
in-the-face, or they could ride out

its one, last, long-suffering
note, now swaybacked, now
milk-mouthed, as if anyone ever got home

on that old, that murdered
mule.

About the Author

Sharmila Voorakkara, a native of New Jersey, earned an M.F.A. in creative writing from the University of Virginia, where she was a Henry Hoyns Fellow. A recipient of a Ruth and Jay C. Halls Poetry Fellowship at the University of Wisconsin, she is now an assistant professor of English at Ohio University. *Fire Wheel* is her first book.

About the Book

Fire Wheel was designed and typeset by Amy Freels Petersen, with help from Melanie Rowand.